DO YOU KNOW THE NAMES OF GOD?

Quiz Part 1

By

Paul Muinde

(Elder Shalom)

Table of Contents

DO YOU KNOW THE NAMES OF GOD?	1
Copyright Information	4
Introduction	5
The Personal Name of God	8
God With Us (Immanuel)	11
How To Use The Rest Of This Book	15
1. The Sovereign LORD	16
2. The Lord That Has Hitherto Helped Us	18
3. The God of Covenant	20
4. The Most High God	22
5. The Strong & Mighty God	24
6. The Living God	25
7. The Jealous God	27
8. The Everlasting God	29
9. The God Who Sees Me	31
10. The All Sufficient God	33
11. The Creator	35
12. The Holy God	37
13. The God of Glory	39
14. The Faithful God	41
15. The Lord Our Maker	43
16. The Lord Our Provider	45
17. The Lord Our Banner	47
18. The Lord Our Healer	49
19. The Lord Our Shepherd	51
20. The Lord Our Peace	53

Answers & Prayers Using the Names of God	55
Further Reading	78
About the Author	79

Do You Know The Names of God? Part 1

Copyright Information

Copyright 2014 Paul Muinde

Revised Edition 2014

Introduction

This is Book 1 in the series on the names of God. Each book will be covering about twenty names of God. The digital versions of the book have an interactive quiz at the end of each chapter. The paperback versions have questions at the end of each chapter and answers at the end of the book.

God's names came through revelation to His people. God used them to reveal His character and nature to the nation of Israel. These names are compound names and they are meant to be descriptive. God created intimacy with the nation of Israel through these revelations.

The nation of Israel would call upon God using specific names in different situations for God to manifest Himself according to the way He had described Himself. The names are transliterated from the Hebrew language into the English alphabet. There are several renderings of some of the names e.g. Yahweh Sabaoth is commonly written as Yahweh Tsebaoth.

The Bible tells us to give thanks and call upon the name of the Lord (Psalm 105:1a) and to make His deeds known. It also says that His name is excellent in all the earth (Psalm 8:9). God makes a promise to promote or to set on high those who have known His name (Psalm 91:14b).

At the "burning bush" God had described Himself to Moses as the God of his father, the God of Abraham, of Isaac and of Jacob (Exodus 3:6). When God was sending Moses to deliver the nation of Israel from bondage in Egypt, Moses asked for God's name so that he could tell the Israelites who had sent him. God told him to say "I AM" or "I AM THAT I AM" had sent him (Exodus 3:14). In Hebrew it is " Ehyeh-Asher-Ehyeh". This has been interpreted in a number of ways. One of them is that God never changes.

God is the same always – hence the present tense. It is also a tautology like 1=1. Since God is infinite it is not fully possible to describe Him. That is why in most cases He reveals Himself by His personal name (Yahweh or Jehovah) followed by an attribute of His character. His personal name as you will see later is derived from the Hebrew verb "to be".

In Hebrew El (capital E) stands for God (capital G) but el (lowercase e) stands for god (lowercase g). There are many constructs of Yahweh's name with the word "El" e.g. Yahweh

El Elyon which means "Yahweh God Most High".

This quiz book series is to help Christians and others who share the Old Testament to meditate on the names of God and know them by heart. This will help believers in their worship of the True and Living God, Yahweh.

In order to gain the most from the quiz, it is necessary to memorize a few names per day e.g. pick three names and meditate on them during the day. Start with those that seem to be familiar or close to your heart. Within a short time, you will know many of them.

During your fellowship with God, start referring to Him by His names and your worship and fellowship will grow richer day by day. Apply His name to your situations. For example when you are in need, worship and acknowledge Yahweh as your Yahweh Yireh (your provider) or Yahweh El Shaddai (your sufficiency). Likewise when you feel lost acknowledge Him as Yahweh Rohi (your Shepherd).

Shalom.

Do You Know The Names of God? Part 1

The Personal Name of God

God has a personal or proper name. It is represented by four Hebrew letters:

This is known as the Tetragrammaton. It is derived from a Hebrew verb "to be".

Hebrew letter	ה	ו	ה	י
Name of letter	He	Waw (sometimes written Vav)	He	Yodh
English letter	H	W	H	Y

Hebrew is read from right to left but English is from left to right, so the name is transliterated to YHWH in English commonly pronounced and even written as Yahweh. This is often seen as a blend between two names YHWH and Hashem (the Name) from which the "a" and "e" are derived. The Jews avoid mentioning or writing the name in full for fear of using it in vain or in blasphemy so they often use Hashem instead.

The third commandment in Exodus 20:7 is that "You shall not take the name of Jehovah (some versions use the LORD) your God in vain. For Jehovah (the LORD) will not hold him guiltless that takes His name in vain." (MKJV)

Because of this fear the Jews preferred to use the name Adon (or Adonai) which means LORD (or my LORD) instead of YHWH. All capital letters were used to avoid confusing it with other types of lords. Thus it appears in some Bible translations (versions) in this form. It stands for sovereign owner of everything. The name "God" is also used, interchangeably, in English Bibles.

It should be noted that YHWH was also transliterated into JHVH from which Jehovah was derived. However it should be noted that the letter "J" in Hebrew is actually pronounced as "Y". It is recorded that the form "Jehovah" started appearing in English Bibles after the 16th century. The 1611 KJV Bible uses the following spellings "IEHOVAH" and "Iehouah" for YHWH. Some scholars therefore recommend the use of YHWH or Yahweh instead.

Psalm 83:8

.. So that men may know that Your name is JEHOVAH (YHWH or Yahweh), that You alone are the Most High over all the earth. (MKJV)

God With Us (Immanuel)

One of the names God used prophesying the coming of Jesus Christ the Messiah (*Yeshua Hamashiac* in Hebrew) is Immanuel. The Prophet Isaiah prophesied the birth of Jesus Christ as Immanuel

*"Therefore the Lord himself shall give you a sign; Behold, a virgin shall conceive, and bear a son, and shall call his name **Immanuel** "* (Isaiah 7:14). The name means "God with us".

Because mankind had fallen into sin through Adam and Eve's disobedience to God's command in the Garden of Eden, God purposed to redeem mankind by visiting the earth Himself. He would be here on earth with us. That was His plan for mankind's salvation.

The angel of the LORD appeared to Mary and prophesied the birth of Jesus Christ as it is recorded in the Gospel of Luke:

*Luke 1:31 And behold! You shall conceive in your womb and bear a son, and you shall call His name **JESUS**.*

*Luke 1:32 He shall be great and shall be called the **Son of the Highest.** And the Lord God shall **give Him the throne of His father David.***

*Luke 1:33 And He shall reign over the house of Jacob forever, and of **His kingdom there shall be no end.***

Luke 1:34 Then Mary said to the angel, How shall this be, since I do not know a man?

*Luke 1:35 And the angel answered and said to her, The Holy Spirit shall come on you, and the power of the Highest shall overshadow you. Therefore also that **Holy One** which will be born of you shall be called **Son of God**.*

Jesus Christ was the one prophesied about by Isaiah as Immanuel (God with us). God called Jesus Christ, His Son and gave Him the throne of David and declared that Jesus' reign shall never end. God had promised David many years ago that his throne would last forever.

2 Samuel 7:16 And your (David's) house and your kingdom shall be made sure forever before you. Your throne shall be established forever.

This was to be fulfilled through Jesus Christ who was a descendant of David since Mary was of the lineage of David but His Father is the Holy Spirit (God). Jesus qualified to redeem mankind. He entered the earth as a man even though He had the Spirit of God. He is the mediator between God and man. He is sometimes referred to as the God-man. He often referred to Himself the Son of Man.

Jesus responded to the Jews with these words:

John 8:58 "Jesus said to them, Truly, truly, I say to you, Before Abraham came into being, I AM!"(MKJV)

The Bible tells us in Romans 11:33

"O the depth of the riches both of the wisdom and knowledge of God; how unsearchable are His judgments and His ways past finding out."

God uses His own counsel (advice) i.e. He advises Himself. For His salvation plan to work He had to enter the earth as a man. For mankind had fallen into sin through one man (Adam) so salvation was to come through one man, Jesus Christ the Messiah (*Yeshua Hamashiac* in Hebrew). *Yeshua* means salvation. Here is a historical summary:

1) Sin entered the world through Adam

Romans 5:12. Therefore, even as through one man sin entered into the world, and death by sin, and so death passed on all men inasmuch as all sinned:

Romans 5:14. But death reigned from Adam to Moses, even over those who had not sinned in the likeness of the transgression of Adam, who is the type of Him who was to come;

2) The wages of sin is death.

Romans 6:23. For the wages of sin is death, but the gift of God is eternal life through Jesus Christ our Lord.

3) Jesus Christ has reconciled us to God.

Romans 5:11. And not only so, but we also rejoice in God through our Lord Jesus Christ, by whom we have now received the reconciliation.

Romans 5:17. For if by one man's offense death reigned by one, much more they who receive abundance of grace and the gift of righteousness shall reign in life by One, Jesus Christ.

Now that we know the personal name of God and the fact that He came to the earth to reconcile mankind to Himself through Jesus Christ – the Messiah, we can now look at the descriptive names of God. These names are usually appended to His personal name to describe His character and His attributes.

How To Use The Rest Of This Book

For best results:

1. Read each chapter and meditate on it. Try to answer the question at the end of the chapter.

2. Check the answer.

3. Pray the prayer and ensure that you memorize the name and meditate on it.

4. You can limit the reading to three (3) names i.e. three chapters at a time.

5. At each reading session, you can start by trying to remember the names you have memorized so far. If you have forgotten, it is better to go back and memorize them before continuing.

6. Within a short time you will be able to remember all the twenty (20) names in this book. This will enrich your prayer life.

1. The Sovereign LORD

"HE'S GOT THE WHOLE WORLD IN HIS HANDS..."

God wants us to know that He is sovereign in every situation. Nothing is outside God's control. What is outside our control is under God's control. What is outside our circle of influence is inside God's circle of influence. God's circle of control and circle of influence have infinite radii. For the non-mathematical, this means the God's circles are boundless.

The Bible tells us that the earth belongs to the Lord and all that is contained in it (Psalm 24:1). The Jews avoided calling God by His personal name (YHWH) preferring to call Him LORD which meant the owner or sovereign.

Do You Know The Names of God? Part 1

Which name below does God use to describe His sovereignty?

A) Yahweh Shalom
B) Yahweh Adonai
C) Yahweh El Shaddai

Check answer on Page 56.

2. The Lord That Has Hitherto Helped Us

"HE IS OUR HELP IN TIMES OF TROUBLE"

The Psalmist tells us that his help comes from the LORD who made the heaven and the earth. He admonishes us not to put our trust in princes and people in whom there is no help. And finally he tells us that happy is he that has the God of Jacob for his help whose hope is in the LORD his God. (Psalm 121:2; 124:8; 146:3; 146:5)

The Children of Israel referred to the Lord with a name signifying that He was the one who had helped them defeat their enemies up to that point in time. In the days of Samuel the prophet, the Philistines came to attack the children of Israel at a place called Mizpeh as they prepared to pray to the Lord. Samuel sacrificed a burnt offering to the Lord and the Lord thundered from heaven and confused the Philistines who were then easily defeated by the children of Israel. Samuel made an altar that place, between Mizpeh and Shen, and gave it a name signifying the Lord had helped up to that point.

Do You Know The Names of God? Part 1

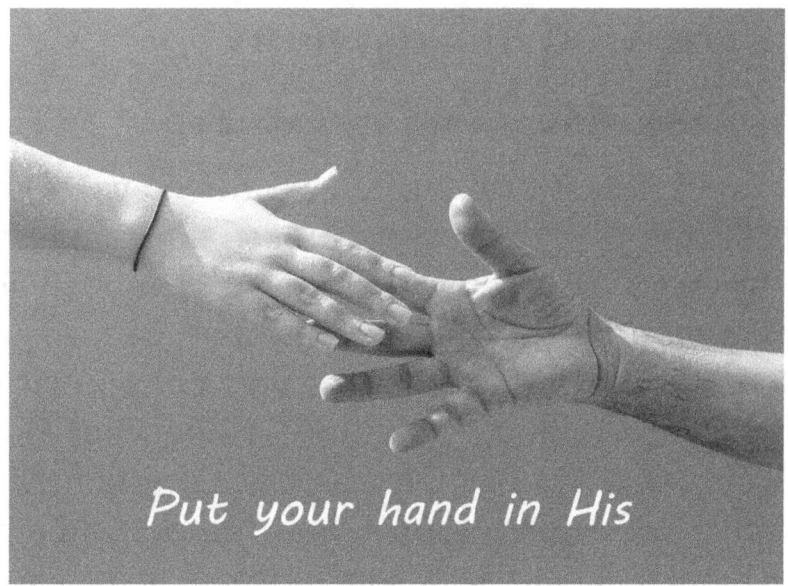

Which name best describes God as the one who has brought us thus far or helped us up to this point? ?

A) Yahweh Nissi
B) Yahweh El Gibbor
C) Yahweh Ebenezer

Check answer on Page 57.

3. The God of Covenant

"HIS PROMISES ARE YES AND AMEN .."

In this world, many treaties have been made and many have been broken due to man's selfishness. The Bible tells us that cursed is everyone that puts his trust in man instead of God. We should first and foremost put our trust in God at all times. He says what He means and means what He says. He has promised that His word will not return to Him without accomplishing what He intended it to do. We can rely on His word. (Jeremiah 17:5; Isaiah 55:11)

He watches over His Word to perform it

God made a covenant with Abraham. He promised Abraham that He would multiply him to be a great nation and that He would give him and his descendants land. God has also made a new covenant with all mankind through Jesus

Christ's crucifixion, death and resurrection. God gives all those who believe in Jesus Christ the right to be called His sons. There is no distinction between male and female. God gives them the gift of salvation, righteousness and eternal life.

Which name does God reveal Himself in to describe the fact that He is a covenant keeping God?

A) Yahweh El Berit
B) Yahweh El Elyon
C) Yahweh El Kanno

Check answer on Page 58.

4. The Most High God

"He's Above All"

One time the Apostle Paul was visiting Athens. He found them worshipping a number of Gods. However one of them drew Paul's attention. He found an altar with an inscription of "to the unknown god". Paul took the opportunity to declare to the Athenians the God that they did not know. He is Yahweh and He is above all gods. (Acts 17:23)

Satan tried to be like God (the Most High) and he was thrown out like lightning.

Isa 14:13-15 For you have said in your heart, I will go up to the heavens, I will exalt my throne above the stars of God; I will also sit on the mount of the congregation, in the sides of the north. (14) I will go up above the heights of the clouds; I will be like the Most High. (15) Yet you shall be brought down to hell, to the sides of the Pit.

There is a specific name that refers to Yahweh as the most high God. Which is it among the following?

A) Yahweh El Elyon
B) Yahweh Rohi
C) Yahweh Yireh

Check answer on Page 59.

5. The Strong & Mighty God

"POWER & MIGHT BELONG TO OUR GOD.."

In God's hand there is power and might (strength). In His hand He makes great and gives strength to all. No one can withstand Yahweh. (1Chronicles 29:12). The Children of Israel were told not to be afraid because the Mighty God was with them. He was going to destroy their enemies (Deuteronomy 7:21-23).

None can contend with the Almighty God

He thunders from Heaven and scatters His enemies

Which of the names of God best describes Him as strong and mighty?

A) Yahweh Mekaddishkhem
B) Yahweh El Olam
C) Yahweh El Gibbor

Check answer on Page 60.

6. The Living God

"THE SOURCE OF ALL LIFE"

Everything that exists was created by God. The word of God tells us that it is impossible to please God without faith. Those that come before Him must first believe that He exists and that He rewards all those that diligently seek Him (Hebrews. 11:6). There are several names which are closely related that speak of God as the one who is there or who is the living God.

Jesus told the Samaritan woman that God is a Spirit and those that worship Him must do so in spirit and in truth (John 4:24). He told Philip, the disciple, that He that has seen Him (Jesus) has seen the Father (John 14:9).

Jesus Christ is the image of the invisible God (Colossians 1:5). In Him dwells the fullness of the Godhead bodily (Colossians 2:9). He is the brightness of God's glory and the express image of His person (Hebrews 1:3). Jesus Christ is the Way, the Truth and the Life. No one comes to the Father except through Jesus Christ (John 14:6). He is the only way to the Living God.

Do You Know The Names of God? Part 1

Which specific reference to God describes Him as the living God?

A) Yahweh El Hai
B) Yahweh Ori
C) Yahweh Sali

Check answer on Page 62.

7. The Jealous God

"Never Worship Idols"

One time King Agrippa gave a speech which was well applauded by the audience saying it was the voice of a god because of his oratory. Because he did not give the glory to God, the Bible says an angel struck King Agrippa down and he was eaten by worms. (Acts 12:21-23). King Nebuchadnezzar was made to eat grass when he gloried (boasted) in himself (Deuteronomy 4:29-33). God does not share His glory with any man (Isaiah 42:8). He has warned creation to worship Him and Him alone. People often worship idols without knowing. An idol is anything that you give credit to when the credit belongs to God.

When you excel in your job and you praise yourself, you become your own idol. If you praise the gift instead of the Giver of the gift, then you are worshipping an idol. Have you ever heard someone say "I don't know what I could have done without you". We should thank God for those He has used to bless us and not elevate them at the expense of crediting (thanking) God for His loving kindness and tender mercies.

Which name describes Yahweh as a jealous God?

A) Yahweh Yisrael
B) Yahweh Hanne'eman
C) Yahweh El Kanno

Check answer on Page 63.

8. The Everlasting God

"THE ETERNAL GOD"

God has no beginning and no end. He does not change (Malachi 3:6). He is not constrained by time and space. He is not constrained by anything. Sometimes He is referred to as the "Ancient of Days" (Daniel 7:9), however He does not get old. He is the same yesterday, today and forever. Space and time are in His hands. The Bible tells us that He declares the end from the beginning i.e. He declares what will happen in the future in advance (Isaiah 46:10). He sees everything in time and space.

Which is the name of God that refers to Him as the Everlasting God?

A) Yahweh El Berit
B) Yahweh El Nose
C) Yahweh El Olam

Check answer on Page 65.

9. The God Who Sees Me

"YOU CAN RUN BUT YOU CANNOT HIDE"

Some people think that they can hide from God. The fact that no human being is seeing you does not mean that God is not seeing you. God sees everything. You may be going through tough times. Everything may seem to be going wrong. God sees it all. You are not alone. Apply His word to your situation. His Truth will set you free. Only the truth that you apply will benefit you.

Nothing is hidden from His sight..

The Bible says the eye of the Lord moves to and fro throughout the earth looking for those whose hearts are loyal to Him that He may show Himself strong on their behalf (2 Chronicles 16:9).

Sarah, Abraham's wife, chased Hagar (her maidservant) away because of her mockery. Hagar ran into the desert where she met the LORD who revealed Himself as the God who sees her.

Which of the descriptive names of God describes Him as the God who sees?

A) Yahweh Ori
B) Yahweh El Roi
C) Yahweh Rohi

Check answer on Page 66.

10. The All Sufficient God

"The God of More Than Enough"

God is self-sufficient. He does not need anyone or anything. That may seem to be strange to some people. Whatever He requires of us or from us is actually for our own good. He requires our obedience and our worship. He revealed Himself to Abraham as the "All Sufficient God" (Genesis 17:1). He required Abraham to walk before Him and to be perfect (complete and holy). Then he would experience God's sufficiency. In the New Testament, the Bible tells us that His grace is sufficient for us (2 Corinthians 12:9). This was primarily being addressed to Paul but it also applies to all believers.

Which of the descriptive names of God describes Him as the All Sufficient God?

A) Yahweh El Shaddai
B) Yahweh Shalom
C) Yahweh Rapha

Check answer on Page 67.

11. The Creator

"EVERYTHING THAT EXISTS WAS MADE BY HIM"

In the beginning God made everything, the heavens and the earth and all that dwells in them. He created everything for Himself. All of creation owes its existence to God the Creator. Creation's response should be worship of the Creator. This worship is realized through believing in and living in obedience to God's Word. It is necessary to obey the whole of God's Word and not just part of it. This same Word will be used to judge creation.

Which of the following names identifies God as the Creator?

A) Yahweh Tsebaoth
B) Yahweh Shammah
C) Yahweh Elohim

Check answer on Page 68.

12. The Holy God

"ONE OF A KIND"

God is holy. The Bible tells us that without holiness no one shall see God (Hebrews 12:14). We are also told to be holy as He is holy (1 Peter 1:16). At first this may seem impossible. This is true if we rely on our own ability. If God expects us to be holy, then it means it is possible for human beings to be holy. One meaning of the word holy is set apart or unique or one of a kind. Christians are to be set apart by the word of God. Jesus Christ prayed to God that His followers would be sanctified through God's truth (John 17:17). Therefore in order to be holy, study the word of God and live it every day.

You do not qualify to be saved by being holy. Indeed all have sinned and come short of the glory of God (Romans 3:23). We are saved by grace through faith in Jesus Christ. It is the gift of God (Ephesians 2:8). Righteousness is also a gift from God. It is imputed upon us. After getting saved you receive grace to pursue peace and holiness (Hebrews 12:14-15).

Do You Know The Names of God? Part 1

Which of the following names identifies God as the Holy God?

A) Yahweh El Kanno
B) Yahweh Hakkadosh
C) Yahweh Ebenezer

Check answer on Page 69.

13. The God of Glory

"HE DOES NOT SHARE HIS GLORY WITH ANYONE"

God deserves all the glory. We should never glory in man. The Bible is very categorical that if anyone is to "glory" or boast they should always glory in God. In fact Christians are instructed to do everything for the glory of God. God has said that He will not share His glory with anyone. When King Agrippa made a well applauded speech, the people said it was not the voice of a man but that of a god. Because he did not renounce what they said and give the glory to God, he was struck down by an angel of the Lord. He was eaten by worms and died (Acts 12:23).

The Heavens Declare His Glory····

Jesus Christ left Christians His earthly glory before returning to Heaven. He then went back and received His heavenly glory. He is seated on the right side of God the Father in Heaven.

Which of the following names identifies God as the God of Glory?

A) Yahweh Hakkavod
B) Yahweh Yireh
C) Yahweh Tsidkenu

Check answer on Page 70.

14. The Faithful God

"HE IS FOREVER FAITHFUL"

God is faithful to those who love Him and to those who keep His commandments. The Bible says up to a thousand generations (Deuteronomy 7:9). Even if a generation was twenty five years, this means God's faithfulness would be for twenty five thousand years! That in essence translates to forever. Faithful is He who called us (1 Thessalonians 5:34a). He will always do what He has promised. The Bible says that through His faithfulness he will not allow us to be tempted beyond our capacity to withstand temptation (1 Corinthians 10:13). This means we have no excuse for sinning. We should never waver in our faith in God for He always delivers on His promises. He treasures His Word.

Do You Know The Names of God? Part 1

Even in the storms of life He is with us...

God will do what He says. The Psalmist had faith in God. He said even if he were to go through the valley of the shadow of death, he would not fear any evil because God was with him (Psalm 23:4).

Which of the following names identifies God as the faithful God?

A) Yahweh Hanne'eman
B) Yahweh El Gibbor
C) Yahweh Hakkadosh

Check answer on Page 71.

15. The Lord Our Maker

"HE IS THE POTTER; WE ARE THE CLAY"

God made us. We have seen that He is our Creator. The Bible compares Him to a potter and human beings as the clay. God is able to mold us a potter molds clay (Jeremiah 8:6). God told the prophet Jeremiah to observe how a potter molds clay. He told Jeremiah that the House of Israel was like clay in His hands.

In this dispensation God rarely forces His will upon us. However, if we yield to His will, He will mold us and make us after Christ's image and likeness. Jesus Christ is the Christian's perfect model.

He is the Potter and we are the clay...

God predestined us to be conformed (made) into the image of His Son (Jesus Christ)

– the first born among many brethren (Romans 8:29). The Bible also describes Jesus Himself as the image of God (2 Corinthians 4:4).

Which of the following names identifies God as our Maker?

A) Yahweh El Hai
B) Yahweh El Kanno
C) Yahweh El Hoseenu

Check answer on Page 72.

16. The Lord Our Provider

"THE LORD WILL PROVIDE AT THE PLACE OF NEED"

When God asked Abraham to sacrifice his son Isaac as a burnt offering, Abraham obeyed. As they were going up the mountain, Isaac observed that his father had carried fire and wood but there was no lamb. So Isaac asked his father where the sacrifice was. His father responded by saying that God would provide for Himself. This could have been the first answer that came to his mind or he probably thought deeply before responding. Whichever the case it was prophetic for God did provide the sacrifice at the time and place of need (Genesis 22:7).

He prepares a table for us in the presence of our enemies...

When God calls us to do something for Him, He always provides the means and resources to accomplish it. In many cases patience is necessary. The promises of God are obtained through faith and patience (Hebrews 6:12).

Which of the following names identifies God as our provider?

A) Yahweh Yeshuatenu
B) Yahweh Yireh
C) Yahweh El Berit

Check answer on Page 73.

17. The Lord Our Banner

"HE CAUSES THEM TO SCATTER IN SEVEN WAYS"

Israel fought with the Amalekites at a place called Rephidim. Moses instructed Joshua to go and fight the Amalekites while he, Aaron and Hur went up a hill where they could see the battle. It so happened that when Moses lifted God's rod, the Israelites prevailed against the Amalekites. However, if he lowered his hands the Amalekites would prevail against the Israelites.

Moses hands were getting tired so Aaron and Hur put stones under his hands to keep the rod high so that the Israelites would continue to win. After winning the battle, Moses built an altar to the Lord at Rephidim (Genesis 17:8-16). He gave the place a name which signified that the Lord would wage war against the Amalekites from generation to generation.

Which of the following names identifies God as our Banner?

A) Yahweh El Shaddai
B) Yahweh Nissi
C) Yahweh Hakkavod

Check answer on Page 74.

18. The Lord Our Healer

"HE HEALS ALL OUR DISEASES"

In the book of Psalms we read that God heals all our diseases (Psalm 103:3). The Psalmist was probably referring to God's promise to the Israelites in the book of Exodus. God had promised to keep sickness away from the Israelites as long as they kept His commandment. He also declared to them that He was the Lord that healed them (Exodus 15:26). He not only heals all our physical ailments but He also heals broken hearts (Psalm 147:3). The Bible also tells us He is also able to heal our land (our situations) when we turn away from sin and pray (2 Chronicles 7:14).

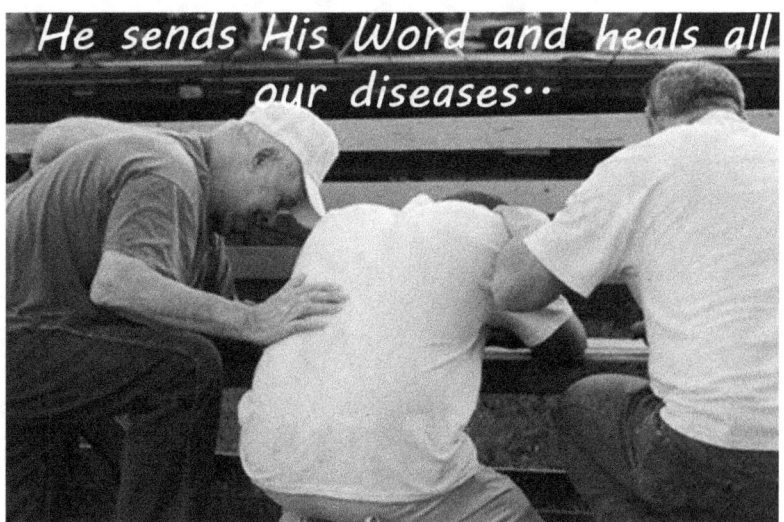

Do You Know The Names of God? Part 1

During Jesus Christ's earthly ministry He preached the gospel of the Kingdom of God everywhere He went, healing all manner of sicknesses and casting out demons. He also declared He had come to heal the broken-hearted among other things (Luke 4:18).

Which of the following names identifies God as our Healer?

A) Yahweh El Kanno
B) Yahweh Rapha
C) Yahweh El Roi

Check answer on Page 75.

19. The Lord Our Shepherd

"He Leads Us In Green Pastures"

The most famous Psalm is the twenty third Psalm. God revealed Himself to David as a shepherd. David being a shepherd was familiar with the characteristics of a shepherd. God often uses what is natural to manifest the supernatural or to explain the supernatural. A shepherd leads the sheep to graze in green pastures, cares for the sheep when hurt. He also protects the sheep from enemies. The shepherds used to lead the sheep from the front (unlike in some other countries) and the sheep used to follow. In fact from a tender age the shepherd taught the sheep to know his voice. This was useful in case they got lost he could call or whistle and they would locate him. That explains Jesus statement when He said that His sheep hear His voice and follow Him (John 10:27).

The Bible also calls those who believe in God, His people and the sheep of His pasture (Psalm 100:3). Psalm 95:7-8 tells believers that they should not harden their hearts when God is speaking to them. Here the Bible refers to believers as the people of His pasture.

Do You Know The Names of God? Part 1

Which of the following names identifies God as our Shepherd?

A) Yahweh Rohi
B) Yahweh Rapha
C) Yahweh El Roi

Check answer on Page 76.

20. The Lord Our Peace

"HE GIVES GRACE TO THE HUMBLE..."

Jesus Christ gave the peace of God to his disciples and all those who would follow after them (John 14:27; John 20:21). The peace of God is beyond all human understanding (Philippians 4:7). This peace is supposed to govern the hearts of believers (Christians). When most people talk about peace, they usually mean the absence of war. However, the peace of God is beyond the absence of war. It means everything being the way it ought to be – just as God meant it to be. This means all needs have been met. There should be no sickness, no bondage, and no fear. It also means total wellness of spirit, soul and body. We may not be experiencing this all the time but it should be our desire and our aspiration in God as the Lord our Peace. God alone gives us that peace. Jesus spoke peace to the turbulent storm in the sea and there was calm. The disciples were astonished (Mark 4:39).

Jesus expects all Christians to be peacemakers. He said "blessed are the peacemakers for they shall be called the sons of God" (Matthew 5:9). The corollary is that as sons of God (Christians), we should be peacemakers.

In the book of James it is stated that the fruit of righteousness is sown through peace by peacemakers (James 3:18). The gospel of Christ is propagated through peace. It is a message of reconciliation (2 Corinthians 5:18). It reconciles us to God and to our fellow human beings. Being justified by faith we have peace with God (Romans 5:1).

Which name identifies God as our Peace?

A) Yahweh Rohi
B) Yahweh Rapha
C) Yahweh Shalom

Check answer on Page 77.

Answers & Prayers Using the Names of God

Answer 1B

Congratulations! That is the right answer:

You can read Genesis 15:2-8 about Yahweh Adonai. In this portion of scripture God is promising Abraham the land that He was to give him. Abraham addresses God by the name Adonai (my LORD) or owner.

You can thank God by saying this short prayer:

Thank You God (Yahweh) for being my LORD. I submit myself to you. All that I am and all that I have belongs to you. I call upon you to reign in my life. I will not worry about anything as long as you remain LORD in my life. In Jesus name I have prayed.

Amen

Answer 2C

Congratulations! That is the right answer:

You can read 1 Samuel 7:12 about Yahweh Ebenezer. It says:

"Then Samuel took a stone, and set it between Mizpeh and Shen, and called the name of it Ebenezer, saying, Hitherto hath the LORD helped us." (KJV)

As we reflect on life we should always acknowledge God as the one who has sustained us from the time we were babies up to now. Some people have gone through more challenges than others. Everyone has had their share. In fact the Bible tells us that even before we were born, God knew us and predestined us to be conformed to the image (likeness) of Jesus Christ (Romans 8:29).

You can thank God by saying this short prayer:

Thank You God (Yahweh) for being my Ebenezer, for being my constant companion, for being with me as I go out and as I come in, as I rise every morning and as I go to rest every evening; in Jesus name.

Amen

Answer 3A

Congratulations! That is the right answer:

You can read the following portion of scripture about Yahweh El Berit.

Deuteronomy 7:9

Therefore, know that Jehovah your God, He is God, the faithful God who keeps covenant and mercy with them that love Him and keep His commandments, to a thousand generations. (MKJV)

You can thank God by saying this short prayer:

Thank You God (Yahweh) for the New Covenant that You have made with me through Your Son Jesus Christ. Thanks for the gift of righteousness through Jesus Christ. Thanks for the gift of salvation. Thanks for Your gift of eternal life in Jesus name.

Amen.

Answer 4A

Congratulations! That is the right answer:

You can read the following portions of scripture about Yahweh El Elyon.

Here are some portions of Scripture:

Psalm 7:17 I will praise Jehovah (the LORD) according to His righteousness, and will sing praise to the name of Jehovah most high. (MKJV)

Psalm 47:2 For Jehovah (the LORD) Most High is awesome, a great king over all the earth. (MKJV)

You can thank God by saying this short prayer:

I acknowledge you Yahweh as the Most High. There has never been another like You. There is none like You and there will never be another like You. You are above all, Yahweh El Elyon. I believe in You in Jesus name.

Amen.

Answer 5C

Congratulations! That is the right answer:

You can read the following portions of scripture about Yahweh El Gibbor (The Mighty God).

Isaiah 9:6 For unto us a child is born, unto us a son is given: and the government shall be upon his shoulder: and his name shall be called Wonderful, Counsellor, The mighty God, The everlasting Father, The Prince of Peace.

Jeremiah 32:18 You show loving-kindness to thousands, and repay the iniquity of the fathers into the bosom of their sons after them. The great, the mighty God, Jehovah of Hosts, is His name,

Jeremiah 32:19 great in wisdom and mighty in work; for Your eyes are open on all the ways of the sons of men, to give every one according to his ways and according to the fruit of his doings.

You can thank God by saying this short prayer:

Thank you God (Yahweh) for being my El Gibbor. You are the Mighty God. According to 2 Chronicles 16:9, You have said that Your eyes move to and fro throughout the earth that You may show Yourself strong on behalf of those whose hearts are loyal to You May You find my heart loyal to you this day and be my strength in Jesus name.

Amen.

Answer 6A

Congratulations! That is the right answer:

You can read the following portion of scripture about Yahweh El Hai.

Psalm 42:2

*My soul thirsts for God, for the **living God**; when shall I come and appear before God? (MKJV)*

You can acknowledge God by saying this short prayer:

I acknowledge you Yahweh as the True Living God. There is no other God beside You. You are welcome to live in my heart always. According to Your Word I am the temple of your Holy Spirit (I Corinthians 3:16). May I live in You always in Jesus name.

Amen..

Answer 7C

Congratulations! That is the right answer:

You can read the following portions of scripture about Yahweh El Kanno also written as Yahweh El Kannah.

*Exodus 20:5 You shall not bow yourself down to them, nor serve them. For I Jehovah your God am a **jealous God**, visiting the iniquity of the fathers upon the sons to the third and fourth generation of those that hate me,*

*Exodus 34:14 For you shall worship no other god. For Jehovah, whose name is Jealous, is a **jealous God**;*

Deuteronomy 4:23 Take heed to yourselves, lest you forget the covenant of Jehovah your God, which He made with you, and make you a graven image, a likeness of anything which Jehovah your God has forbidden you.

*Deuteronomy 4:24 For Jehovah your God is a consuming fire, a **jealous God**.*

You can acknowledge God by saying this short prayer:

I acknowledge you Yahweh as El Kanno. Remember mercy upon me today for every instance where I have worshipped idols without knowing. Forgive me for often times glorying in Your gifts rather than in You. I pray this in Jesus name.

Amen.

Answer 8C

Congratulations! That is the right answer:

You can read the following portions of scripture about Yahweh El Olam.

*Genesis 21:33 And Abraham planted a tree in Beer-sheba, and called there on the name of Jehovah, the **everlasting God**. (MKJV)*

Psalm 93:2 Your throne is established of old; You are from everlasting. (MKJV)

Isaiah 26:4 Trust in Jehovah forever; for in the LORD JEHOVAH is everlasting strength. (MKJV)

You can acknowledge God by saying this short prayer:

I acknowledge you Yahweh as the Everlasting God. You have no beginning and no end. You are the same yesterday, today and forever. I thank You for giving everlasting life to be with You forever in Jesus name.

Amen.

Answer 9B

Congratulations! That is the right answer:

You can read the following portions of scripture about Yahweh El Roi.

*Genesis 16:13 Hagar asked herself, "Have I really seen God and lived to tell about it?" So she called the LORD, who had spoken to her, "A **God Who Sees.**" (GNB)*

*Genesis 16:14 That is why people call the well between Kadesh and Bered "The Well of the Living One **Who Sees Me**." (GNB)*

You can thank God by saying this short prayer:

I thank You Yahweh El Roi for always watching over me. May I always sense you indwelling presence wherever I go and at all times in Jesus name.

Amen.

Answer 10A

Congratulations! That is the right answer:

You can read the following portion of scripture about Yahweh El Shaddai.

Genesis 17:1 And when Abram was ninety-nine years old, Jehovah appeared to Abram and said to him, I am the Almighty God (Yahweh El Shaddai)! Walk before Me and be perfect.

You can thank God by saying this short prayer:

I thank You Yahweh El Shaddai for being my sufficiency through Your grace. You are the one who has met and continues to meet every need in my life. I thank You in Jesus name.

Amen.

Answer 11C

Congratulations! That is the right answer:

You can read the following portion of scripture about Yahweh Elohim.

Genesis 1:1 In the beginning God (Elohim) created the heavens and the earth.

Elohim is a plural form of Eloha. Various explanations have been made as to why the plural form is used. Although the noun is plural God is One. Probably the plural is used in some instances to describe the fact that He manifests Himself in many ways yet He is One. Similarly as evidenced in this book He has many attributes but they all belong to the One God.

You can acknowlege God by saying this short prayer:

I acknowledge You Yahweh Elohim. You are the One who made everything including myself. I thank You for Your plan for me in Jesus name.

Amen.

Answer 12B

Congratulations! That is the right answer:

You can read the following portions of scripture about Yahweh Hakkadosh.

*Isaiah 5:16 But Jehovah of Hosts is exalted in judgment, and God the **Holy One** is sanctified in righteousness.(MKJV)*

You can acknowledge God by saying this short prayer:

I acknowledge You Yahweh Hakkadosh. You are holy and you require me to be holy. Help me by your grace to be holy in Jesus name.

Amen.

Answer 13A

Congratulations! That is the right answer:

You can read the following portions of scripture about Yahweh Hakkavod.

Psalm 29:3 The voice of Jehovah is on the waters; the God of glory thunders; Jehovah is above many waters. (MKJV)

You can acknowledge God by saying this short prayer:

I acknowledge You Yahweh Hakkavod. May Your manifested presence accompany me always and everywhere I go. Father of Glory I pray that You grant me Your Spirit of wisdom and revelation and help me experience Your power in my life according to Your Word in Ephesians 1:17-18. This I pray in Jesus name.

Amen.

Answer 14A

Congratulations! That is the right answer:

You can read the following portion of scripture about Yahweh Hanne'eman.

*Deuteronomy 7:9 Therefore, know that Jehovah your God, He is God, the **faithful God** who keeps covenant and mercy with them that love Him and keep His commandments, to a thousand generations.*

You can thank God for His faithfulness by saying this short prayer:

I thank You Yahweh Hanne'eman for your faithfulness that endures for a thousand generations for those who love You and keep Your commandments. I pray for grace to be faithful to what You have called me to accomplish today and in this life. This I pray with thanksgiving and believing in the precious name of Jesus Christ.

Amen.

Answer 15C

Congratulations! That is the right answer:

You can read the following portion of scripture about Yahweh Hoseenu.

Psalm 95:6 Oh come, let us worship and bow down; let us kneel before Jehovah our maker. (MKJV)

You can thank God for making you in this short prayer:

I thank You Yahweh Hoseenu for making me. You have made me fearfully and wonderfully according to Your Word (Psalm 139:14). You have attended to every detail of my being. I appreciate You for who You are. Help me to bring glory and honor to Your Holy name in Jesus Christ's name.

Amen.

Answer 16B

Congratulations! That is the right answer:

You can read the following portions of scripture about Yahweh Yireh (Jireh).

Genesis 22:14 Abraham named that place "The LORD Provides." And even today people say, "On the LORD's mountain he provides." (GNB)

You can acknowledge God for being your provider in this short prayer:

I thank You Yahweh Yireh for providing for all my needs. I believe Your Word that says in Psalm 34:10 *"The young lions lack, and suffer hunger; but those who seek Jehovah shall not lack any good thing."*

I also acknowledge Your Word in Psalm 84:11 that says *"..You shall not withhold any good thing from those who walk uprightly before You "*. I pray that You will continue to lead me in the paths of righteousness for Your name's sake that I may be a beneficiary of this wonderful promise in Jesus Christ's name.

Amen.

Answer 17B

Congratulations! That is the right answer:

You can read the following portions of scripture about Yahweh Nissi.

Exodus 17:13 And Joshua defeated Amalek and his people by the edge of the sword.

Exodus 17:14 And Jehovah said to Moses, Write this, a memorial in a book, and set it in the ears of Joshua, that I will utterly put out the remembrance of Amalek from under heavens.

*Exodus 17:15 And Moses built an altar, and called the name of it **Jehovah My Banner**. (MKJV)*

You can acknowledge God as Your Banner in this short prayer:

I thank You Yahweh Nissi. You are my Banner against my foes. You are the one who shows Yourself strong for me. The battles and the oppositions I face in life are not mine but they are Yours as You declared for the nation of Israel when You fought for them.

May You always fight for me all the battles in my life and give me the victory always. Thank You Abba Father in Jesus name I have prayed.

Amen.

Answer 18B

Congratulations! That is the right answer:

You can read the following portions of scripture about Yahweh Rapha.

*Exodus 15:26 And he said, If you will carefully listen to the voice of Jehovah your God, and will do that which is right in His sight, and will give ear to His commandments, and keep all His Laws, I will put none of these diseases upon you, which I have brought upon the Egyptians; for I am **Jehovah who heals you**. (MKJV)*

Psalm 103:2 Bless Jehovah, O my soul, and forget not all His benefits;

Psalm 103:3 who forgives all your iniquities; who heals all your diseases; (MKJV)

You can acknowledge God as Your Healer in this short prayer:

Lord, You are my Yahweh Rapha – the Lord my Healer. I thank You for healing my diseases in Jesus name.

Amen.

Answer 19A

Congratulations! That is the right answer:

You can read the following portion of scripture about Yahweh Rohi.

Psalm 23:1 Jehovah is my Shepherd; I shall not want.

Psalm 23:2 He makes me to lie down in green pastures; He leads me beside the still waters.

You can acknowledge God as Your Shepherd in this short prayer:

Lord, You are my Yahweh Rohi. I thank for leading me in green pastures and in the paths of righteousness. I thank You for taking care of me as a shepherd takes care of his sheep. Help me to hear Your voice in Jesus name I pray.

Amen.

Answer 20C

Congratulations! That is the right answer:

You can read the following portions of scripture about Yahweh Shalom.

Judges 6:22 And when Gideon saw that He was the Angel of Jehovah, Gideon said, Alas, O Lord God! Because I have seen the Angel of Jehovah face to face.

Judges 6:23 And Jehovah said to him, Peace to you. Do not fear. You shall not die.

*Judges 6:24 Then Gideon built an altar there to Jehovah, and called it **Jehovah-shalom**. It is yet in Ophrah of the Abiezrites to this day.*

You can acknowledge God as Your Peace in this short prayer:

Yahweh Shalom, You are my peace. You calmed the troubled sea. I invite You to calm every storm in my life. I invite You to impart Your Shalom that surpasses all human wisdom. I pray this in Jesus name.

Amen.

Further Reading

This is Part 1 in the series. Part 1 is also available on Kindle. The Kindle version is interactive. If you get the wrong answer, you are given another chance to state the right name of God in the quiz. If you get it right you are allowed to proceed to the next chapter. This makes it easy to remember the Hebrew attribute names of God.

More descriptive names of God (YHWH) are available in Part 2.

If you would like more information about the series you can email the author at abouthashem@gmail.com

About the Author

Paul Muinde loves studying God's word, singing His praises and sharing His word with others. Paul believes that the body of Christ needs daily edification. Believers should build each other in the faith through reading and applying God's word.

Believers should also worship God through psalms and spiritual songs and pray always for God's will to be done on the earth as it is done in Heaven. Paul was a member of the advisory board of a local church for many years where he was better known as Elder Shalom. He is currently pastoring a local church with his wife Rose in Kenya.

www.ingramcontent.com/pod-product-compliance
Lightning Source LLC
LaVergne TN
LVHW011738060526
838200LV00051B/3236